Table **of Contents**

Essential Question

How can other perspectives help us evaluate the world?

Recognizing
Author's
Point of View

Recognizing Author's Point of View

Credits
Editor: Jeffrey B. Fuerst
Contributing Editors: Joanne Tangorra, Brett Kelly
Creative Director: Laurie Berger
Art Directors: Melody DeJesus, Kathryn DelVecchio-Kempa, Doug McGredy, Chris Moroch
Production: Kosta Triantafillis
Director of Photography: Doug Schneider
Photo Assistant: Jackie Friedman

Photo credits: Cover D, Cover F: © Everett Collection Inc/Alamy; TOC A, Page 4B: © Bettmann/CORBIS; Page 2: ©North Wind Picture Archives; Page 5B: © CORBIS; Page 7: Library of Congress; Page 9: © Granger, NYC

Illustrations: Marcin Piwowarski: Page 3 and Pages 13–19; Tom Sperling: Pages 23–29

Permissions: "I, Too" from *The Collected Poems of Langston Hughes* by Langston Hughes, edited by Arnold Rampersad with David Roessel, Associate Editor, copyright © 1994 by the Estate of Langston Hughes. Used by permission of Alfred A. Knopf, an imprint of the Knopf Doubleday Publishing Group, a division of Random House LLC. All rights reserved.

Excerpt from *My Name is America: The Journal of Wong Ming-Chung* by Laurence Yep. Copyright © 2000 by Laurence Yep. Reprinted by permission of Scholastic Inc. Excerpt from *Zora And Me.* Copyright © 2011 by Victoria Bond and T.R. Simon. Reproduced by permission of the publisher Candlewick Press, Inc., Somerville, MA. Excerpt from *Esperanza Rising* by Pam Munoz Ryan. Copyright © 2000 by Pam Munoz Ryan. Reprinted by permission of Scholastic Inc.

© Benchmark Education Company, LLC. All rights reserved. No part of this publication may be reproduced or transmitted in any form or by any means, electronic or mechanical, including photocopy, recording, or any information storage or retrieval system, without permission in writing from the publisher. Printed in Mexico. 10789/0120/065406
ISBN: 978-1-4900-9208-9

Tips for Text Annotation

As you read closely for different purposes, remember to annotate the text. Use the symbols below. Add new symbols in the spaces provided.

Symbol	Purpose
underline	Identify a key detail.
★	Star an important idea in the margin.
① ② ③	Mark a sequence of events.
magma	Circle a key word or phrase.
?	Mark a question you have about information in the text. Write your question in the margin.
!	Indicate an idea in the text you find interesting. Comment on this idea in the margin.

Your annotations might look like this.

3   Madison argued for a strong central government. At the time, the thirteen states had a lot of power to govern themselves. This made it hard for a national government to collect taxes or create a military. After months of discussion and debate, and many compromises the delegates decided on a final document. They mostly followed Madison's Virginia Plan and established a stronger federal government.

What power did the sides have?

Find out more about the Virginia Plan

4   Madison also helped write a series of newspaper articles called the Federalist Papers. These articles helped persuade readers to accept the new Constitution.

5   Soon after, Madison helped create the Bill of Rights. These are the first ten amendments, or additions, to the

LEXILE® is a trademark of MetaMetrics, Inc., and is registered in the United States and abroad.

E-book and digital teacher's guide available at benchmarkuniverse.com.

BENCHMARK EDUCATION COMPANY
145 Huguenot Street • New Rochelle, NY • 10801

Toll-Free 1-877-236-2465
www.benchmarkeducation.com
www.benchmarkuniverse.com

3

Notes

I Hear America Singing

by Walt Whitman

Walt Whitman (1819–1892) was an American poet whose long, expansive lines broke with poetic tradition as he celebrated the self and the individual American spirit.

I hear America singing, the varied carols I hear,
Those of mechanics, each one singing his as it
    should be blithe and strong,
The carpenter singing his as he measures his
    plank or beam,
The mason singing his as he makes ready for
    work, or leaves off work,
5 The boatman singing what belongs to him in his
    boat, the deckhand singing on the
    steamboat deck,
The shoemaker singing as he sits on his bench,
    the hatter singing as he stands,
The wood-cutter's song, the ploughboy's on his
    way in the morning, or at noon intermission
    or at sundown,
The delicious singing of the mother, or of the
    young wife at work, or of the girl
    sewing or washing,
Each singing what belongs to him or her
    and to none else,
10 The day what belongs to the day—at night
    the party of young fellows, robust, friendly,
Singing with open mouths their strong melodious
    songs.

I, Too

by Langston Hughes

*The poems of Langston Hughes (1902–1967),
an innovator of "jazz poetry" during the
Harlem Renaissance, claim a space for the
African American experience and a voice in
the "song" of America. "I, Too" is Hughes's response to Whitman, a
poet he considered to be one of his major influences.*

I, too, sing America.

I am the darker brother.
They send me to eat in the kitchen
When company comes,
5 But I laugh,
And eat well,
And grow strong.

Tomorrow,
I'll be at the table
10 When company comes.
Nobody'll dare
Say to me,
"Eat in the kitchen,"
Then.

15 Besides,
They'll see how beautiful I am
And be ashamed—

I, too, am America.

Notes

Gold Country

An excerpt from *The Journal of Wong Ming-Chung: A Chinese Miner, California, 1852*

by Laurence Yep

The Journal of Wong Ming-Chung (published in 2000) is historical fiction written in the form of a journal. It is told from the perspective of "Runt," a bookish young teen who travels alone to California from his native China to help his uncle search for gold during the California Gold Rush. These are excerpts from his journal entries written soon after he arrives.

June 18

San Francisco, or First City

1 The Golden Mountain is stranger, scarier, funnier, sadder and more wonderful than I ever imagined. Now that I am here I will use only the American calendar.

2 When we got off the ship, I thought I was in the middle of a forest. Except I could hear the ocean. Then I realized the tall poles were the masts of ships. I was surrounded by hundreds of empty boats. They jam the harbor like fish in my village pond. I bet I could have walked from one deck to another across the bay.

3 I didn't see any sailors. Instead, I saw laundry hanging from lines as if people were using the boats as houses. Then I saw one ship that literally had a house built on top of it. Maybe all the sailors had left their ships to find gold too.

4   Big, loud machines were pounding logs vertically into the mud a half-kilometer from shore. Real houses perched on top of logs that had already been driven in. Men and machines were filling in the shoreline to make more space. In some places, they weren't even bothering to move the ship, but were just filling the dirt around it. Blessing[1] would have loved the machines.

5   First City nestles at the foot of steep hills between the shore and the hillsides. A few houses lie scattered on the slopes. Instead of building on the hills, they're expanding into the water.

6   Though it's summer, the air is as chilly here as winter back at home.

7   I have to stop now. They're calling for us to register.

1 Blessing—Runt's older brother, still in China

This is San Francisco during the Gold Rush.

June 20

Somewhere northeast of San Francisco

8   This morning I boarded a smaller boat by myself. It traveled across a broad bay and then through a series of smaller ones to a river.

9   The boat is crammed with miners traveling to the gold country. They clump together in groups, each of which talks a different language.

10   Because I couldn't find water, I couldn't write, so I got bored. There were some other Chinese on board, but they were busy gambling. They wouldn't have allowed me to join even if I had money.

11   So I wound up drifting over to the side of the boat to look at the water. Suddenly, a fish leapt out of the water. Its sides shone in the sun so it looked like a silver arrow. It was so lovely it would be a shame to eat it.

12   When the fish splashed back into the water, I felt a nudge in my side.

13   I spun around to defend myself. I saw an American boy with hair the color of fire. He looked to be about the age of Blessing. He grinned and pantomimed fishing.

14   I guess he had been thinking some of the same things.

15   Through signs, we learned each other's names. It took a while to work out his name because his name was in reverse. In China, your family name is the most important thing, so we put our family's name first and our personal name second. Americans must think the opposite, because they put their personal names first and their family names last. Strange. His personal name is Brian. His family name is Mulhern.

Head of Auburn ravine California

Thousands came to California hoping to strike it rich during the Gold Rush. The Chinese called the area "Golden Mountain."

16   He's just as curious about me as I am about him. After a while, I forgot about how strange he looked.

17   Unfortunately signs got us only so far. So then he took out what I thought was a stick. It ended in a point with some black stuff. He called it a pencil.

18   He was able to write on the deck without a brush and ink. I don't think I will ever give those up since the writing is nicer to look at, but the pencil is handier when you're traveling.

19   Then, through pictures and signs, I learned that he is not an American. He comes from a country called Australia. I'm embarrassed to say that I have never heard of it. If I understand him right, his country is to the south of China.

20   I wish we had studied more about the world. However, our teacher felt that China was the most civilized country in the world. Why should we study any other place? We had learned about the Golden Mountain only because our clansmen were going there.

21   I admired his pencil so much that he gave it to me. I tried not to take it but he insisted. My new friend has a big heart.

22   I am writing this with my new writing implement. No more ink sticks. No more inkwells. No more finding water.

Remember to annotate as you read.

Notes

Annie's New Homeland

1   "We're coming into New York Harbor!"

2   Fifteen-year-old Annie perked up at her brother's words. The voyage by steamship from Ireland to the United States had been long and difficult. It was a bitter, cold day in January 1892, but she and her two brothers rushed to the deck. They gaped at the welcoming Statue of Liberty.

3   Annie thought of her parents back home and tears came to her eyes. They had scraped together enough money for the three oldest children to make this journey to America, the land of opportunity. Annie shuddered to think of all those thousands of people in Ireland who had perished when the crops failed and famine struck. She was one of the lucky ones, and she felt grateful, nervous, and excited all at the same time.

4   The steamship docked, but before the passengers were allowed ashore, they had to pass through customs at Ellis Island. They waited in long lines in the crowded Registry Room to be examined by doctors to see if they had any physical problems. Annie knew that if she failed the exam, she would be sent back to Ireland. She held her breath until the doctor said, "You're in good health, young lady. Next!" Her brothers passed, too. Another long line took them to a customs officer who looked over their documents. Fortunately, everything was in order, and they were allowed to enter the United States. Finally! Annie heaved a sigh of relief.

5   Gathering their belongings, the three headed bravely into New York City. Annie would look for work as a cook or a maid, while her brothers would begin the dangerous work of building bridges and railroads. Life would not be easy, but Annie knew they'd survive and contribute to their new homeland.

BuildReflectWrite

Build Knowledge

Based on this week's readings, write down some similarities and differences between the first person speaker of a poem and the first person narrator of a story.

Similarities and Differences	First Person Point of View (Poem)	First Person Point of View (Story)
Similarity #1		
Similarity #2		
Difference #1		
Difference #2		

Reflect

How can other perspectives help us evaluate the world?

Based on this week's texts, write down new ideas and questions you have about the essential question.

_____

_____

_____

_____

_____

Writing to Sources

Informative/Explanatory

Choose one of the poems from your first Short Read. In an informational essay, describe how its narrator's point of view differs from that of Wong Ming-Chung in "Gold Country." Support your essay with details and evidence from the text.

Remember to annotate as you read.

Notes

Justice in Eatonville

An excerpt from *Zora and Me*

by Victoria Bond and T. R. Simon

Zora and Me (2010) is a fictional account of the early life of Zora Neale Hurston (1891–1960), the African American author, anthropologist, and folklorist. Hurston was a prominent figure of the Harlem Renaissance, and renowned as a great storyteller. Zora and Me takes place in Eatonville, Florida, the first incorporated African American town in the United States, where Hurston grew up. The novel, narrated by Zora's friend Carrie, follows the two fourth-grade girls and their friend Teddy as they attempt to solve a murder mystery. In this excerpt from Chapter 25 of the novel, Zora and Carrie confront Joe Clarke, the town sheriff and owner of the general store. The girls tell him what they suspect about the incident and the people involved: Gold, a beautiful woman who comes back to town on the arm of a white suitor; Ivory, a turpentine worker who arrives one day in search of Gold; and Mr. Pendir, an elderly man whom Zora believes to be "half-gator" and "half-man."

1   The following afternoon, we went to Joe Clarke's store.

2   We knew we had a mission, and we knew we couldn't breathe a word about it.

3   I thought about Gold. No matter how bad she felt now, she couldn't change what had happened.

4   When we got to Joe Clarke's store, the usual cast of characters stood on the porch interrupting one another. Mr. Clarke was leaning against a post as usual, but he didn't look right as rain. He leaned like a powerful tree taking a long overdue rest. The look in his eyes was far from peaceful.

5   Zora spoke. "Can I talk to you, Mr. Clarke?"

6   The chorus went silent.

7   "'Course you can," he said. He seemed to welcome the distraction.

8   "Don't do it, Joe," someone called out. "They only want to take you for more licorice!"

9   "No, we don't." Zora said it so calmly that Mr. Clarke could tell she was dead serious.

10   He ushered us into the store and led us to the small office in the back. The desktop was covered in papers— receipts, bills of lading, and long sheets of numbers in rows. I looked at the shiny varnished legs of the desk. They held the shape of sturdy branches.

11   Zora dove into the conversation like skipping rope; she just jumped right in. "I overheard you talking with Gold out by the Loving Pine."

12   Mr. Clarke stared at Zora for a moment, taken aback. "What did you say, child?"

13   "I heard you and Gold talking in the woods on Tuesday. We went to see her that evening to tell her Ivory had been looking for her. We wanted to help lay his spirit to rest." Zora looked at Mr. Clarke. He was still just staring at her.

14   She pressed on. "Then Gold starts wailing and tells us how jealous her white man is, that white man she goes with in Lake Maitland." Zora paused. "She thinks he maybe killed Ivory."

15   Joe Clarke was at a loss for words. Zora, sensing his shock, talked more and faster.

Notes

16　　"We haven't told a soul, Mr. Clarke. Not until yesterday when we saw old Mr. Ambrose by the lagoon. I told him everything 'cause he helped bring me into this world, and you can trust someone who done a big thing like that for you. And he said you could trust him, too. He told me to tell you that he knew you would do justice in Eatonville. He wanted you to know that he'll do justice in Lake Maitland."

17　　Joe Clarke sat back in his chair, looking winded. None of us spoke. Then he stood up and turned his back to us for a long minute. When he turned around again, he looked like his old self.

18　　I was so relieved that I burst into a grin, but Zora wasn't so quick to end our talk. She wanted more answers. Now that we knew who Gold and Ivory were, and how Joe Clarke knew them, and maybe who had taken Ivory's life, there was one piece of the puzzle still missing. And Zora, determined to know everything, demanded the final answer.

19   "What about Mr. Pendir? Did he want to be a gator more than a man?"

20   Mr. Clarke looked at us thoughtfully before answering.

21   "Yes and no," Joe Clarke said, squinting. "Pendir got dealt more hurt than he knew how to play. He lost his mama and daddy early on. His mama's family were poor sharecroppers and they didn't need another mouth to feed, so he was raised working for white folks, but like a slave, not like a child. He grew up feeling like a whipping post. He was grown when he heard about Eatonville and came here, hoping there was enough work from colored folks that he'd never have to deal with white folks again. At first folks tried to bring him into the circle of town life, but he just couldn't put his hurt and mistrust away. He knew how to work wood, but he never learned how to be friendly with folks, and never learned how to let folks be friendly with him. He kept to himself and after a while folks got used to hiring him for work, but otherwise leaving him be."

22   Mr. Clarke stood and stretched his big bones. "This desk right here, Mr. Pendir made it for me. He was blessed with the power to take plain wood—scraps too small to be worth much to anyone—and carve them and shape them and paint them into something else."

23   He reached into a drawer and drew out a lion mask so detailed that Zora and I gasped. "Mr. Pendir breathed life into wood. When his fears threatened to swallow him up, he faced them down with the masks he made. His art scared off his fear."

24   I thought about Mr. Pendir missing his mama and daddy, and I wondered if I had anything beautiful to make inside myself that would still my own fears. Then I thought about Gold. She and Mr. Pendir had something in common. They both felt afraid and cheated by the cards life had dealt them, but they took that fear and channeled it in different ways. Mr. Pendir took his fear inside and locked himself into a room alone. Gold hid her fear inside and walked away from where she came from and everything she knew. Both of them ended up alone.

25   The bad things that happen to you in life don't define misery—what you do with them does. When Mr. Pendir and Gold could have chosen connection, they chose solitude; when they could have brought loving themselves to loving someone else, they wore masks instead and shunned love's power. You can't hide from life's pain, and folks that love you would never expect you to.

26   Zora and I sat with that a moment. Joe Clarke's lips spread across his face in a closed-mouth smile. It was a sad smile, but reassuring.

27   "I'm going to do justice, girls, but sometimes justice works better in silence. You didn't do wrong to tell me and Mr. Ambrose. But don't tell anyone else what you know. Let justice take its course now."

28   When we reappeared on the front porch of Joe's store, our pockets and mouths full of licorice sticks, the men of Eatonville broke into an uproar.

29   "Joe, you let these two little girls sucker you into giving them treats again," one man said.

30   "Watch out, Joe," said another. "These two gonna leave you bankrupt!"

31   "Giving don't got a thing to do with going bankrupt," Joe Clarke answered. "Holding back does."

Remember to annotate as you read.

Notes

Zora Neale Hurston

1   The Zora in the novel *Zora and Me* is based on a real person—the author Zora Neale Hurston. Like the character, the real Zora was strong and confident. She was born in Alabama in 1891 but spent her childhood in Florida. Zora eventually left the South. She was bound for Harlem, an African American neighborhood in New York City. When she arrived, she had only $1.50 and one published story to her name. However, she persevered with her writing. Over the next thirty years, she published four novels, two books of folklore, an autobiography, and a number of short stories and plays. She won many awards for her work.

2   Hurston was a rare kind of person who could walk into a room and command immediate attention. She was smart and amusing, and people liked her. Her storytelling cast a spell on the audience. One friend recalled that she had "the gift of walking into hearts."

3   Hurston didn't finish high school till her mid-twenties. She then went on to graduate from college, where she studied anthropology, the science of human culture and beliefs. As part of her studies, she developed an interest in folklore, stories such as *Cinderella* and *Jack and the Beanstalk*, which are passed down from parents to children.

4   She spent years collecting and publishing the folklore and stories of southern Americans. Without her work, many of these traditional stories might have been lost forever. Her own stories and novels, however, were based on her life growing up as an African American in the rural South.

5   Hurston eventually returned to her beloved Florida, where she died in 1960. Her gravestone reads, "Zora Neale Hurston: A Genius of the South."

BuildReflectWrite

Build Knowledge

In your own words, explain Joe's last line from the *Zora and Me* excerpt:
"Giving don't got a thing to do with going bankrupt," Joe Clarke
answered. "Holding back does." What does this say about Joe's character?

Interpreting *Zora and Me*

Reflect

How can other perspectives help us evaluate the world?

Based on this week's texts, write down new
ideas and questions you have about the
essential question.

_____

_____

_____

_____

_____

Writing to Sources

Narrative

Write a series of journal entries from
Zora's point of view, in which you
describe your encounter with Mr. Clarke.
Use details and evidence from "Justice in
Eatonville" to support your writing, and
use "Gold Country" as a model for how
you should write your journal entries.

Remember to annotate as you read.

Notes

Asparagus

An excerpt from *Esperanza Rising*

by Pam Muñoz Ryan

Esperanza Rising (2000) tells the story of a thirteen-year-old girl who is living a life of privilege in Mexico when tragedy strikes and her family loses everything. As a result, they are forced to migrate to California during the Great Depression of the 1930s and become farmworkers. This excerpt from "Los Duraznos" ("Peaches"), a chapter toward the end of the book, reveals what life is now like for the story's characters: Esperanza Ortega, who is struggling to adapt to her hardscrabble new life; Hortensia (the Ortega family's housekeeper from Mexico); Isabel (a young relative of Hortensia's); and Miguel (Hortensia's son, age seventeen).

1   A week later Esperanza put yet another bundle of asparagus on the table after work. The tall and feathery asparagus plants seemed to be as unrelenting as Isabel's desire to be queen. The workers picked the spears from the fields and a few days later, the same fields had to be picked again because new shoots were already showing their heads. And Isabel talked of nothing else, except the possibility of wearing the winner's crown of flowers on her head.

2   "I hate asparagus," said Isabel, barely looking up from her homework.

3   "During grapes, you hate grapes. During potatoes, you hate potatoes. And during asparagus, you hate asparagus. I suppose that during peaches, you will hate peaches."

4   Isabel laughed. "No, I love peaches."

5   Hortensia stirred a pot of beans and Esperanza took off the stained apron she wore in the sheds and put on another. She began measuring the flour to make *tortillas*. In a few minutes, she was patting the fresh dough that left her hands looking as if she wore white gloves.

6   "My teacher will choose the Queen of the May this week," said Isabel. Her entire body wiggled with excitement.

7   "Yes, you have told us," said Esperanza, teasing her. "Do you have anything new to tell us?"

8   "They are making a new camp for people from Oklahoma," said Isabel.

9   Esperanza looked at Hortensia. "Is that true?"

10   Hortensia nodded. "They announced it at the camp meeting. The owner of the farm bought some army barracks from an old military camp and is moving them onto the property not too far from here."

11   "They get inside toilets and hot water! And a swimming pool!" said Isabel. "Our teacher told us all about it. And we will all be able to swim in it."

12   "One day a week," said Hortensia, looking at Esperanza. "The Mexicans can only swim on Friday afternoons, before they clean the pool on Saturday mornings."

13   Esperanza pounded the dough a little too hard. "Do they think we are dirtier than the others?"

14   Hortensia did not answer but turned to the stove to cook a *tortilla* on the flat black *comal*[1] over the flame. She looked at Esperanza and held her finger to her mouth, signaling her not to discuss too much in front of Isabel.

15   Miguel walked in, kissed his mother, then picked up a plate and a fresh *tortilla* and went to the pot of beans. His clothes were covered in mud that had dried gray.

16   "How did you get so dirty?" asked Hortensia.

17   Miguel sat down at the table. "A group of men showed up from Oklahoma. They said they would work for half the money and the railroad hired all of them." He looked into his plate and shook his head. "Some of them have never even worked on a motor before. My boss said that he didn't need me. That they were going to train the new men. He said I could dig ditches or lay tracks if I wanted."

18   Esperanza stared at him, her floured hands in midair. "What did you do?"

1 *comal*—Spanish for griddle

19   "Can you not tell from my clothes? I dug ditches." His voice was sharp but he continued eating, as if nothing were wrong.

20   "Miguel, how could you agree to such a thing?" said Esperanza.

21   Miguel raised his voice. "What would you have me do instead? I could have walked out. But I would have no pay for today. Those men from Oklahoma have families, too. We must all work at something or we will all starve."

22   A temper Esperanza did not recognize raged to the surface. Then, like the irrigation pipes in the fields when the water is first turned on, her anger burst forth. "Why didn't your boss tell the others to dig the ditches?!" She looked at the dough she was holding in her hand and threw it at the wall. It stuck for an instant, and then slowly slid down the wall, leaving a darkened trail.

23   Isabel's serious eyes darted from Miguel to Esperanza to Hortensia. "Are we going to starve?"

24   "No!" they all answered at the same time.

25   Esperanza's eyes were on fire. She stamped out of the cabin, slamming the door, and walked past the mulberry and the chinaberry trees to the vineyard. She hurried down a row, then cut over to another.

26   "Esperanza!"

27   She heard Miguel's voice in the distance but she didn't answer. When she got to the end of one row, she moved up to another.

28   "Anza!"

29   She could hear him running down the rows, catching up with her.

30   She kept her eyes on the tamarisk trees in the far distance and walked faster.

31   Miguel eventually caught her arm and pulled her around. "What is the matter with you?"

32　"Is this the better life that you left Mexico for? Is it? Nothing is right here! Isabel will certainly not be queen no matter how badly she wants it because she is Mexican. You cannot work on engines because you are Mexican. We have gone to work through angry crowds of our own people who threw rocks at us, and I'm afraid they might have been right! They send people back to Mexico even if they don't belong there, just for speaking up. We live in a horse stall. And none of this bothers you? Have you heard that they are building a new camp for Okies, with a swimming pool? The Mexicans can only swim in it on the afternoon before they clean it! Have you heard they will be given inside toilets and hot water? Why is that, Miguel? Is it because they are the fairest in the land? Tell me! Is this life really better than being a servant in Mexico?"

33　Miguel looked out over the grapes where the sun set low on the horizon, casting long shadows in the vineyard. He turned back to her.

34　"In Mexico, I was a second-class citizen. I stood on the other side of the river, remember? And I would have stayed that way my entire life. At least here, I have a chance, however small, to become more than what I was. You, obviously, can never understand this because you have never lived without hope."

35　She clenched her fists and closed her eyes tight in frustration. "Miguel, do you not understand? You are still a second-class citizen because you act like one, letting them take advantage of you like that. Why don't you go to your boss and confront him? Why don't you speak up for yourself and your talents?"

36 "You are beginning to sound like the strikers, Esperanza," said Miguel coldly. "There is more than one way to get what you want in this country. Maybe I must be more determined than others to succeed, but I know that it will happen. *Aguántate tantito y la fruta caerá en tu mano.*"

37 The words stopped her as if someone had slapped her face. Papa's words: Wait a little while and the fruit will fall into your hand. But she was tired of waiting. She was tired of Mama being sick and Abuelita being far away and Papa being dead. As she thought about Papa, tears sprang from her eyes and she suddenly felt weary, as if she had been clinging to a rope but didn't have the strength to hold on any longer. She sobbed with her eyes closed and imagined she was falling, with the wind whooshing past her and nothing but darkness below.

38 "Anza."

39 *Could I fall all the way back to Mexico if I never opened my eyes again?*

40 She felt Miguel's hand on her arm and opened her eyes.

41 "Anza, everything will work out," he said.

42 Esperanza backed away from him and shook her head, "How do you know these things, Miguel? Do you have some prophecy that I do not? I have lost everything. Every single thing and all the things that I was meant to be. See these perfect rows, Miguel? They are like what my life would have been. These rows know where they are going. Straight ahead. Now my life is like the zigzag in the blanket on Mama's bed. I need to get Abuelita here, but I cannot even send her my pitiful savings for fear my uncles will find out and keep her there forever. I pay Mama's medical bills but next month there will be more. I can't stand your blind hope. I don't want to hear your optimism about this land of possibility when I see no proof!"

43   "As bad as things are, we have to keep trying."

44   "But it does no good! Look at yourself. Are you standing on the other side of the river? No! You are still a peasant!"

45   With eyes as hard as green plums, Miguel stared at her and his face contorted into a disgusted grimace. "And you still think you are a queen."

46   The next morning, Miguel was gone.

47   He had told his father he was going to northern California to look for work on the railroad. Hortensia was confused and worried that he would leave so suddenly, but Alfonso reassured her. "He is determined. And he is seventeen now. He can take care of himself."

48   Esperanza was too ashamed to tell anyone what was said in the vineyard and she secretly knew Miguel's leaving was her fault. When she saw Hortensia's anxiety, Esperanza felt the heavy responsibility for his safety.

49   She went to Papa's roses and when she saw the first bloom, her heart ached because she wished she could run and tell Miguel. *Please, Our Lady,* she prayed, *don't let anything happen to him or I will never be able to forgive myself for the things I said.*

Remember
to annotate
as you read.

Notes

British English and Me

1   Last summer I flew to Great Britain to visit my cousin Fletcher and his family. When they picked me up at the London airport, it was already afternoon, so Fletcher said, "You must be starving. Why don't we go get some grub?"

2   Visions of grubs—slimy white worms—danced through my head. Who would eat them? Well, it turns out that "grub" is British slang for "food." I scratched my head and commented that I thought we both spoke the same language—English! Apparently we do speak the same basic language, but some words differ.

3   As we walked to the restaurant, Fletcher and I window-shopped. Fletcher was interested in a pair of trainers—which are running shoes, by the way—but when he saw the price, he said, "Goodness! Those cost the bomb!" His mother kindly translated that the shoes were expensive.

4   Then we had to wait for the lollypop man—a crossing guard—to give us the okay to walk across the street.

5   At the restaurant, Fletcher took one look at the expression on my face as I read the menu and offered to help me with suggestions about what to order. "Try the bangers and mash," he encouraged.

6   *Why not?* I thought, and was pleased when I received sausages and mashed potatoes.

7   When we finished, the streets were full of people going to a football match, which is actually soccer in American English. I couldn't believe my good fortune when I found out that Fletcher's parents had purchased tickets!

8   By the time we returned to their apartment that night, I was quite knackered—that's "tired out" to you Yanks, but I was getting the hang of British English!

BuildReflect**Write**

Build Knowledge

How are Esperanza's and Miguel's points of view about being in America similar? How are they different? Write down your ideas on the chart below. Include specific quotes of dialogue to support your statements.

Esperanza's Point of View	Miguel's Point of View

Reflect

How can other perspectives help us evaluate the world?

Based on this week's texts, write down new ideas and questions you have about the essential question.

_____

_____

_____

_____

_____

Writing to Sources

Opinion

In "Asparagus," Esperanza expresses a negative view of the "American Dream," which is the idea that America is a place of fairness and opportunity for everyone. Do you agree with Esperanza's point of view? In an essay, support your opinion with evidence from "Asparagus" and from at least one other reading from this unit.

Support for Collaborative Conversation

Discussion Prompts

Express ideas or opinions . . .

When I read _____, it made me think that _____.

Based on the information in _____, my [opinion/idea] is _____.

As I [listened to/read/watched] _____, it occurred to me that _____.

It was important that _____.

Gain the floor . . .

I would like to add a comment. _____.

Excuse me for interrupting, but _____.

That made me think of _____.

Build on a peer's idea or opinion . . .

That's an interesting point. It makes me think _____.

If _____, then maybe _____.

[Name] said _____. That could mean that _____.

Express agreement with a peer's idea . . .

I agree that _____ because _____.

I also feel that _____ because _____.

[Name] made the comment that _____, and I think that is important because _____.

Respectfully express disagreement . . .

I understand your point of view that _____, but in my opinion _____ because _____.

That is an interesting idea, but did you consider the fact that _____?

I do not agree that _____. I think that _____ because _____.

Ask a clarifying question . . .

You said _____. Could you explain what you mean by that?

I don't understand how your evidence supports that inference. Can you say more?

I'm not sure I understand. Are you saying that _____?

Clarify for others . . .

When I said _____, what I meant was that _____.

I reached my conclusion because _____.

Group Roles

Discussion Director:
Your role is to guide the group's discussion and be sure that everyone has a chance to express their ideas.

Notetaker:
Your job is to record the group's ideas and important points of discussion.

Summarizer:
In this role, you will restate the group's comments and conclusions.

Presenter:
Your role is to provide an overview of the group's discussion to the class.

Timekeeper:
You will track the time and help keep your peers on task.

Making Meaning with Words

Word	My Definition	My Sentence
confront (p. 12)		
implement (p. 9)		
justice (p. 15)		
melodious (p. 4)		
optimism (p. 28)		
perspective (p. 6)		
privilege (p. 22)		
reassuring (p. 18)		
solitude (p. 18)		
unrelenting (p. 22)		

Lexile 660L–850L

Build Knowledge Across 10 Topic Strands

Government and Citizenship

Character

Life Science

Point of View

Technology and Society
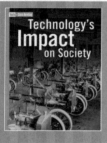

Theme

History and Culture

Earth Science
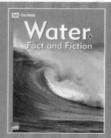

Economics
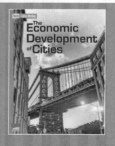

Physical Science

Benchmark
UNIVERSE.COM™

BENCHMARK EDUCATION COMPANY

Grade 5 • Unit 4

ISBN 978-1-4900-9208-9

9 781490 092089